Original title:
The Ocean's Song

Copyright © 2025 Creative Arts Management OÜ
All rights reserved.

Author: Tobias Winslow
ISBN HARDBACK: 978-1-80581-682-9
ISBN PAPERBACK: 978-1-80581-209-8
ISBN EBOOK: 978-1-80581-682-9

Nautical Notations

A fish in a tux, how absurd,
It twirls and it swirls, quite disturbed.
Seashells are giggling, watch them dance,
While crabs hold a conga, what a chance!

The seagulls are gossiping, oh my!
Who stole the last fry? Was it that guy?
The waves clink glasses, salute the tide,
With shrimps doing limbo, what a ride!

Symphonies of Saltwater

Whales hum in harmony, so loud,
While dolphins jump through, quite proud.
Barnacles join in, scratching their heads,
While jellyfish bob like well-fed beds.

Clams recite poetry under the moon,
Their verses are silly, but they croon.
Starfish throw parties, with ten claps,
But who brought the snacks? Just a few wraps!

Crescendo of the Coastline

Sandcastles yell, 'We are bold!'
But waves sneak in, their stories told.
The crabs wear sunglasses, what a sight,
They strut along the shore, day and night.

Seashells whisper secrets, shh, don't shout,
While fish throw a party, there's no doubt.
With seaweed confetti drifting around,
Even the tide can't help but astound!

Undercurrent of Dreams

Starfish dream big, of sailing far,
While sea turtles plot under a star.
The octopus juggles, quite a feat,
While fish ask, 'What's for lunch?' – A treat!

Mermaids giggle with fish in tow,
They trade funny tales from below.
With bubbles that pop like party balloons,
The sea holds laughter, like timeless tunes.

The Call of the Cliffs

Up on the cliffs, seagulls squawk,
They steal your fries, it's quite a shock.
The fishermen laugh, their nets get wet,
While surfers wipe out in the salty fret.

The lighthouse wobbles, lighting the way,
As fish tease the prawns, they dance and sway.
A crab in a tux, oh what a sight,
He waves hello with delight, not fright.

Waves of Wandering Souls

The waves roll in, a silly dance,
As jellyfish float in a weird romance.
They tickle the toes of beachgoers near,
While sandcastles fall, bringing forth a cheer.

A dolphin dons shades in the sun's bright glow,
While starfish play cards, putting on a show.
A seaweed monster steals a lost shoe,
Oh, the ocean's filled with wonders anew!

Nautical Echoes

The sailor shouts, 'Where's my rum?'
His parrot just laughs, it's all so dumb.
A wave springs up, a splashy jest,
The boat rocks with joy, quieted at best.

Cranky old octopus plays the drums,
While fish in tuxedos dance to the thumps.
A clam sings high, with a voice of gold,
Its pearls once hidden, now proudly told.

Tranquil Tides

The tides roll in with a sleepy yawn,
Seashells giggle till the break of dawn.
A whale jumps high, but slips with a splash,
While starfish at twilight join in a bash.

The moon takes a dip, all silver and sly,
While crabs in their shorts blink up at the sky.
As waves whisper stories, soft and light,
The ocean keeps laughing through day and night.

Surf's Serene Soliloquy

Waves dance like clowns, so spry,
Seagulls swoop down, oh my!
Belly flops bring a splashy cheer,
As saltwater tickles without fear.

Boardshorts jive in the salty breeze,
Sunscreen flings with sticky ease.
Tanning on the sand with a quirky grin,
Only to forget where the cool drinks been!

Crabs do the cha-cha along the shore,
While fish throw parties, and then some more.
A beachball hovers like a friendly ghost,
And sunscreen tubes become the utmost boast!

Seashells whisper secrets of old,
While beach towels unfold tales untold.
In this sunny spot, laughter can't cease,
As we search for treasure, or maybe just peace.

Voices of the Vastness

Splashing water sings a silly tune,
Mermaids giggle beneath the moon.
A dolphin sneezes, much to our glee,
While crabs have a race—who will it be?

The tide comes in with a playful shove,
Scooting sandcastles like a little dove.
Seashells argue over who's the best,
While the tide tickles the sand with a jest.

Oceans roar; oh what a scene,
As octopuses juggle, turning routine.
Fished out the salad for lunch today,
And now it swims far, far away!

Sunburned noses, oh what a sight,
Chasing beach balls from morning till night.
Waving at sailors lost on their route,
While we sip smoothies and give a loud shout!

Siren's Serenade

With scales so bright they light the night,
The fish all gather round for delight.
A mermaid sings, she starts to sway,
But dolphins just laugh and swim away.

Her voice is sweet but quite absurd,
As crabs join in with a sideways herd.
They dance and twirl, a silly sight,
While seaweed waves with all its might.

Rhythm of the Deep

Bubbles pop like tiny drums,
The fish all groove, oh how it hums!
A turtle spins, a whale does flip,
While octopuses take a dip.

With jellyfish twirls in shiny glow,
They start a party, everyone's in the flow.
But watch your feet, don't step on a sting,
Or else you'll whirl like a wacky fling!

Ballad of the Brine

In salty froth, the sea stars laugh,
They play hide and seek, on their own behalf.
A clam sings low, a sea snail hums,
While pelicans fly, flapping their thumbs.

The jelly's jiggles cause quite the scare,
As seahorses gossip without a care.
A fish in a tux, what a goofy start,
He twirls his tail and steals the heart!

Echoes of the Sea

Whale calls boom like bass guitar,
The seaweed sways near and far.
Anemones giggle, they wave good cheer,
While seagulls squawk, 'Get outta here!'

A crab with shades struts down the sand,
Sipping seafoam like it's just grand.
With surfboards made of driftwood sleek,
They ride the waves and click their beaks.

Lullaby of the Lighthouse

The lighthouse stands, it starts to hum,
A seagull's dance, oh what a bum!
With beams that guide both ship and fish,
It dreams of making quite a dish.

The waves they crash, they tumble and twist,
The lighthouse spins, it can't resist.
The barnacles laugh and roll with glee,
As lightbulbs wink—hey, look at me!

A foghorn's sound, a splendid roar,
The sailors chuckle, can't take it anymore.
Each beam, a joke, each wave, a play,
As lantern flies chase the night away.

So here's to the light that's funny yet wise,
Filling the night with glowing surprise.
In clamored seas where laughter reigns,
The lighthouse giggles through all the rains.

Chants of the Current

The currents swirl, a cheeky tease,
They tug at boats like playful knees.
A crab sings loud, a fish joins in,
While starfish laugh, their arms all spin.

With underwater jokes that never land,
The jellyfish flap and make a band.
Each bobbing bubble tells a tale,
Of turtles racing, oh what a sale!

From coral reef to sandy beach,
The currents chant, but rarely preach.
They whisper secrets, run and glide,
While octopi dance in waves of pride.

So come and listen, oh what a treat,
To giggles deep in the salty beat.
Where every wave hums its own refrain,
And fish turn rowdy, bursting with gain.

The Sea's Embrace

The sea's a hug that's big and wide,
It sways with fish, and they just hide.
A dolphin jumps, its grin so bright,
Sprays water everywhere in sheer delight.

Its waves they bicker, push and shove,
While crabs have a meeting, hand in glove.
The seaweed dances, getting in line,
As clownfish wear stripes, looking divine.

The salty air carries giggles and cheers,
As surfers ride waves, confronting their fears.
They tumble and twist, splash with pride,
The sea embraces, holding each tide.

So take a dip, and don't forget,
The sea's allure, your funny duet.
In laughter and waves, we all partake,
In a watery world, the best of a shake.

Waves in Harmony

The waves they sing a silly tune,
Making clowns of whales beneath the moon.
With splashes loud, they play their game,
And blame the wind for all their fame.

A crab conducts the surf and sway,
The gulls join in with a somber play.
Each swell promotes a hilarious fuss,
As boats doze off, claiming no muss.

A whale's deep chuckle, a tide's light cheer,
In joyful rhythms, we find them here.
While surfers laugh at their bumpy ride,
The ocean echoes, 'Come join my tide!'

So float along on waves of glee,
In jest and jive, let's all agree.
In every ripple, there's laughter bright,
Where waves unite, both day and night.

Tide's Tuneful Dance

The wave went splashing with a cheer,
Seaweed swayed, a green veneer.
Crabs joined in with tap-tap feet,
While seagulls bobbed to the beat.

A clam sang high, a fish sang low,
Each creature danced, putting on a show.
Jellyfish floated like a balloon,
Bopping along to a carefree tune.

Shells clinked together, a rhythmic sound,
While starfish flipped all around.
The tide pulled back with a whoosh and a wink,
As everyone paused for a quick drink!

At sunset, they bowed with glee,
An ocean crew as funny can be.
In watery worlds where laughter's the law,
They giggled and laughed at it all with awe.

Melody of Moonlit Waters

Under the moon, the waves do sway,
Fishies grin as they find their way.
Octopuses play a prank or two,
Sneaking past with a bubble or a goo.

The night is bright, full of flair,
With crabs in tuxedos, dashing with care.
Starfish sparkle like diamonds in blight,
While sharks have fun, hiding in sight.

Whales whistle tunes that make you smile,
One makes a splash, running a mile.
The dolphins giggle with flips so grand,
Each wave carrying laughter to shore and sand.

As the sea sings under stars on display,
The goofy fish dance, come what may.
In the moonlit depths, the joy's not for naught,
It's a concert of silliness, at the right spot.

Dolphins' Delight

Dolphins leap with a splashy grin,
Doing flips like they're in a spin.
Waves on their backs give them a thrill,
As they frolic with joy, and time stands still.

A fishy friend tells a cheesy joke,
While sea turtles chuckle and croak.
The barnacles laugh, holding on tight,
As the dolphins flip in sheer delight!

They race the boat, quick as a wink,
Leaping high, barely stopping to think.
A silly seal joins in the chase,
Wobbling along with a goofy face.

When twilight arrives, the fun doesn't cease,
The dolphins chatter, "Oh, can't we have peace?"
Yet one more jump, and their glee loudly shouts,
The sea is their playground, full of playful bouts.

Songs of the Shore

Seagulls squawk, a chorus so bright,
As crabs skitter, oh what a sight!
Shells are tapping, out of the sand,
While kids on the beach wave their hands.

The breeze carries songs of joy and cheer,
Picnics underway, bring me a beer!
With sandcastles built that wobbly sway,
The laughter rings as the sun fades away.

A starfish attempts to take center stage,
Dancing awkwardly, but full of rage.
"Oh please," the waves laugh, "just come take a bow,"
While onlookers chuckle, "What a sight now!"

As night falls down, the tides will hum,
The ocean whispers, "Are you having fun?"
And with each wave that crashes and rolls,
The shore joins in, joining their souls.

Waves of a Forgotten Voyage

Once I sailed on a rubber duck,
With a crew of cats and a piece of luck.
We raided the shores for lost treasure,
Found only old socks! Oh, what a pleasure.

The captain squawked, "Hoist the sail!"
While the fish shot past like a tiny whale.
We danced on waves, oh, what a sight!
Until we hit a mermaid's bubble fight.

We played tag with the seagulls in flight,
Laughed as their squawking filled the night.
They stole our snacks, those feathered thieves,
Leaving behind only salty leaves.

Then came a kraken who wanted our hats,
We offered him tuna, he preferred the chats.
So down we went, with giggles galore,
To share jokes with creatures from the ocean floor.

Mysteries of the Distant Dunes

At the shore a crab wore a tiny hat,
Chasing the seagull, oh imagine that!
He declared himself king of the sandcastles,
While the gull just laughed, caught in its wrassles.

The tide pulled back, revealing old shoes,
Each pair a story of sunburned blues.
With a wink and a nudge, we tried them all,
Pretended to dance, had a sandball.

A dolphin played hopscotch on the foam,
Each leap a giggle, it felt like home.
But a wave crashed in, and splashed us around,
We rolled with laughter, lost, not found.

As sunset painted the sky bright and bold,
The crab called a truce, a hand we hold.
We shared our snacks, a feast so grand,
In the mysteries of dunes, we made our stand.

Whispers of the Tide

If you listen close, you'll hear the whispers,
Of clams making jokes, and fish with whiskers.
They tell tales of sailors who sang off tune,
While mermaids flip-flopped beneath the moon.

One fish pranked a crab, tied up its claws,
While another took selfies with gaping jaws.
With bright colored scales, they shimmered and shone,
In this underwater world, we weren't alone.

A seal brought snacks from an ocean café,
Complaining about his workday, oh what a day!
He served us seaweed sushi with a twist,
Topped with a laugh you couldn't resist.

Then came a shark, dressed in a suit and tie,
Said, "I'm off to a meeting, oh my, oh my!"
We cheered him on as he swam away,
In the whispers of the tide, we laughed all day.

Melodies Beneath the Waves

Bubbles sing sweetly in the coral band,
A lobster plays drums, oh isn't it grand?
With dolphins on flutes and a shrimp on guitar,
Together they strum to the beats from afar.

They played a tune that made turtles dance,
Even a slowpoke starfish took a chance.
Crabs did a jig, while the clams kept the beat,
The fish all swirled, moving their feet.

An octopus DJ spun shells in the air,
Everyone laughed, forgetting their cares.
With seaweed confetti and laughter galore,
We partied so hard, our shells got sore.

Then bubbles popped, the party was done,
But the melodies lingered, oh what fun!
As the tide rolled in, we waved goodbye,
Happy memories swirling 'neath the sky.

Seagull Sonnet

A seagull swoops down, quite a sight,
With fries in its beak, it takes flight.
It squawks for its friends, in the sun's glow,
Who knew a bird could steal food like a pro?

They stare at our picnic, plotting a raid,
With eyes like a toddler, unafraid.
But oh, they're just feathers and flappy things,
In the end, it's my lunch that really sings!

Moving Melodies of the Marina

A boat drifts along with a wobble and sway,
The captain's lost dollars—a drink gone astray!
With every small wave, it's a bounce and a giggle,
As fish flip their tails, just to tease and wiggle.

The pelicans dance, quite a comical scene,
With fishy swirls in their beaks, oh so keen.
And sailors with snacks, dropping crumbs at the line,
While a crab sidesteps by, looking oh-so divine!

Trills of the Tidepools

Among the tidepools, creatures take pride,
A starfish with sunglasses, and crab by its side.
With shells like a castle, they pose and they strut,
As kids stomp around, thinking they're hot stuff.

The sea anemones wiggle, like they're in a dance,
While clams close their shells; they won't take a chance.
But a cheeky little shrimp makes a dash for the sand,
With a wink and a wave, he's in high demand!

Soundwaves of Serenity

On the shore, where the waves crash with cheer,
A dog chases shells, and the laughter is near.
The tide brings a rhythm, a boogie, a sway,
While a toddler builds castles that wash away.

The sun sits in a sky, all glitter and gleam,
As seagulls squabble, they form quite the team.
With each goofy stumble and sandy retreat,
We all cheer for the ocean, life's silliest beat!

Nocturne of the Starry Waters

Bubbles rise and fish do dance,
In a seaweed hat, the crab takes a chance.
The clownfish chuckles at a shrimp's loud joke,
While the octopus hides in its polka-dot cloak.

A starfish twirls in a darngood way,
Playing hide and seek with a smooth, shiny ray.
The sea turtle laughs, with a friendly wink,
While the blowfish blows up just to drink.

Seahorses gallop, quite out of sync,
As they sip on seaweed smoothies and think.
The jellyfish jigs, all colorful and bright,
Doing a boogie in the glow of the night.

The Call of the Marine Realm

Splish-splash goes the dolphin, a true acrobat,
Doing flips for the fishes, 'Oh, where's my hat?'
The squid tells stories of the things he's seen,
While the sea cucumber dreams of being a queen.

A hermit crab wearing a new fancy shell,
Practices rhymes; oh, he does it so well!
The pufferfish giggles at a sea turtle's chat,
Knocking over a clam with a playful spat.

Underwater, the seagrass swings and sways,
As fish hum tunes in amusing ways.
A conch shell plays DJ, throwing a rave,
With all the cool critters, oh, what a wave!

Crescendo of the Nautical Night

The waves clap hands, oh what a sight,
As mermaids sing till the fall of night.
A fish with a mustache tells jokes old and bold,
While the crabs play cards with some shiny gold.

Dancing plankton shine, a twinkling light,
As all the sea creatures gather for a bite.
Anemones giggle at the playful seal,
While the grouper whispers, 'What's the big deal?'

The swordfish shows off his shiny new blade,
As sea stars are knitting, a cozy cascade.
With laughter and joy, they all join the fun,
Under the moonlight, till the night is done.

Ballads of the Moonlit Waves

A crab sings ballads, a star in his eyes,
While sea urchins cheer, what a grand surprise!
The otters keep giggling, flippin' around,
In their bubble bath, just splashing down.

The whales are belting tunes, deep and low,
While seagulls listen, putting on a show.
A flounder lands jokes with a flip and a spin,
As a porcupine fish joins in with a grin.

Squid's got his band, playing tunes so sweet,
While the barnacles move to the rhythmic beat.
Corals laugh softly as they sway in the breeze,
In the depths of the sea, just doing as they please.

Windswept Whispers

The seagulls squawk in silly flight,
They steal my fries, oh what a sight!
With salty breezes playing tricks,
I'll hide my snacks from feathered pricks.

The waves are laughing, splish and splash,
As I attempt a daring dash.
But oh, I stumble, fall with grace,
And leave behind a wet embrace.

With laughter bouncing off the pier,
The ocean's jokes are loud and clear.
I toss a shell, it rolls away,
It seems the tide has come to play.

So here I stand, my hair a mess,
The ocean's humor, I confess.
With every wave, a giggle flows,
As I trip along, my joy just grows.

Echoing Estuaries

The boats all bob like silly ducks,
While fishermen are out of luck.
Their nets are tangled, what a scene!
They wave at me, 'Oh, not so keen!'

Crabs dance sideways, with a twist,
I swear they practice to assist.
A jellyfish floats by with flair,
And suddenly, I'm in mid-air!

The fisherman jumps to grab a line,
But trips on seaweed, oh divine!
He lands with quite a splashing sound,
While all the fish just swim around.

In tidal pools, the sea stars wink,
They share their stories, sip and drink.
The echoes laugh, they know the fun,
In estuaries where tides just run.

Harmony of the Horizon

With sun hats on, we surf the breeze,
Each wave a chance to laugh with ease.
A dolphin jumps, strikes a pose,
While careless surfers risk their toes.

The sunset plays a warm charade,
As beach balls bounce, it's quite the parade.
Sandcastles rise with royal grins,
Only to fall when the tide begins.

The stars appear, the night is bright,
And fish are flashing, quite a sight!
We sing along, hearts full of cheer,
The horizon's music, loud and clear.

With every laugh, the night grows old,
The stories of the waves are told.
In harmony, we share our dreams,
Wrapped in laughter, or so it seems.

The Dance of Drifting Boats

On drifting boats, we sway and spin,
With pirate hats and goofy grins.
The anchor's gone, we drift away,
While seagulls cry, 'Now come and play!'

We sing sea shanties, quite off-key,
Making the fishes laugh with glee.
The oars are lost, but we don't care,
Just float along, light as the air.

The starfish giggle on the sands,
As we pretend to steer with hands.
The tides are guiding our grand jest,
On waves of laughter, we're truly blessed.

So here we float, a merry crew,
With every splash, our joy renews.
In this grand dance, we find our home,
A sea of laughter where we roam.

Glistening Galleons

Sailing ships with jiggly sails,
Bringing back the smell of snails,
Swabbing decks with bubblegum,
All the pirates dance and hum.

Mermaids laugh, they splash and play,
Offering us fishy buffet,
Grinning crabs do the cha-cha,
As the sea sways like a grandma.

Whales join in with big, loud tunes,
While squids make ink for funky cartoons,
The gulls are adding silly screams,
Sailing away with all our dreams.

Reflections on the Water

Oh the fish, they played tricks so sly,
Wearing hats and ties that fly,
Jumping high for a giggle spree,
While the jellyfish served us tea.

I saw a turtle with shades on tight,
He danced in the moon, what a funny sight,
Sardines were having a wild parade,
With a conch shell bandit serenade.

The waves chuckle, make ripples of joy,
As crabs cartwheel, what a plucky ploy,
Each splash brings a smile, whimsy's their art,
Nature's jesters, right from the heart.

Serene Shores' Soliloquy

On the shore, the seagulls bicker,
Stealing fries—they're such a sticker,
The sand's a blanket, oh so fine,
But watch your toes, they might just whine!

The waves compose a merry tune,
Adding giggles under the moon,
Starfish tossing jokes like stones,
Crabs trying to laugh in funny tones.

A clam told me he didn't care,
Whether pearls are rare, or just a dare,
With sandcastles filled with giggling mice,
Nothing compares to the ocean's spice!

Oceanic Overture

A dolphin with a tiny hat,
Rides the waves—imagine that,
Jellyfish in a conga line,
Even sharks have joked, "This food's divine!"

The seaweed sways with a playful twist,
Whispering secrets no one could miss,
Barnacles snicker, they cling and cling,
As crabs throw a barbecue fling.

A fishy duo sings out of tune,
Mimicking stars in the bright blue moon,
Every splash a giggle in disguise,
The watery world wears fun-filled skies.

Journey Through the Blue

Waves are giggling, splashing at my toes,
A dolphin dances, strikes a pose!
Seashells chuckle, hiding in the sand,
"Come play with us!" they wave a hand.

The fish are gossiping, what a scene,
"Did you hear about that mermaid queen?"
Seagulls squawk with laughter, flapping wide,
Her royal fin got tangled in the tide!

Crabs in tuxedos shuffle on parade,
Strutting sideways, oh, what a charade!
The starfish giggle, pillow soft and bright,
"Join our party! We're the best tonight!"

With jellyfish jelly and laughter galore,
We'll boogie through waves—not a single bore!
In this realm where fun is awash,
We ride the waves, and oh, what a swash!

Rhythms of the Riptide

In the surf, a crab finds his groove,
Dancing sideways, he's on the move!
Barnacles snicker, stuck to their rock,
"Who needs a dance floor? We'll just mock!"

Waves hop and skip with a bubbly cheer,
Tickling toes as they disappear.
Seashells sing, in a shell-like tone,
Saying, "Join in! You're never alone!"

A fish slides by wearing a bright bowtie,
"Have you seen Bob? He's flying high!"
Laughter echoes, hearty and bright,
As the tide sways left, then bounces right!

Bubble blowers making a splashy show,
While seaweed twirls in the undertow.
It's a comedy under the sun's bright eye,
Where the nautical jokes just float by!

Crescendos at Dusk

As the sun dips down, waves start to prance,
Crickets chirp, and the sea starts to dance.
A sea otter strums on a clam-shell guitar,
Singing notes that float near and far!

Moonlit laughs bounce from wave to shore,
Octopi juggling—what a grand tour!
Seahorses wearing tiny top hats,
Are hosting a gala with musical spats!

The turtles waltz, in a slow, grand parade,
Twisting and turning, their shells displayed.
Underneath, fish play a game of charades,
"Guess what I am!"—the laughter cascades.

With a puff of wind and a bubble or two,
Frogs join in, with their hopping boo-hoo.
As stars twinkle bright in the ocean's embrace,
The night sings a laughter-filled, rhythmic grace!

Twilight's Tranquility

The tide whispers jokes in a salty breeze,
Seashells snicker, "Oh, please, just tease!"
Crabs in sunglasses lounge in the sun,
"Nothing to do, just bask and have fun!"

Stars start arriving, one by one,
Shining like diamonds; the best party's begun.
A whale with a top hat swims on through,
"Care for a dip? There's room for you!"

Bubbles pop like laughter in the air,
Waves weave stories without a care.
The sea foam giggles, suddenly a splash,
Creating tales in a bubbly flash!

As twilight settles and the day starts to close,
Fish join the chorus in joyful prose.
Even the seaweed sways, dancing along,
In this whimsical world, where we all belong!

Breezy Harmonizations

Bubbles rise, fish tickle toes,
A mermaid sneezes, and off she goes.
Seagulls squawk a silly tune,
While crabs dance under the light of the moon.

Sandcastles crumble, giggles soar,
As kids chase waves that lap the shore.
Sandy buckets become hats of fun,
While jellyfish play tag, on the run.

Waves crash loudly, a comical fight,
Starfish refuse to share the limelight.
The sun sets slowly, giving a show,
Even the tide can't help but glow.

Funny tales of the sea unfold,
In every splash, a memory told.
So grab your flippers, come dance along,
With laughter echoing, we all belong.

Song of the Seagrass

Seagrass sways, a dance so bright,
Fish swim by, playing hide-and-seek right.
Crabs wearing sunglasses, ready to strut,
Jellyfish giggle, saying, 'What a glut!'

Shells chatter gossip, secrets they keep,
Starfish complain, they're losing sleep.
Turtles with surfboards, aiming for style,
Ride the waves, with a cheeky smile.

Octopuses juggle, keeping in sync,
While stingrays play hopscotch, in a blink.
Flippers do flips, hearts take flight,
In this underwater world, all feels right.

With seaweed hair doing the cha-cha,
Mermaids cheer on, 'You're a superstar!'
So dive down deep, let laughter ring,
For in the sea, joy is the real king.

Unfurling Waves of Harmony

Waves unfurl with a gentle splash,
Seashells giggle, creating a clash.
Fish wear bowties, ready to dine,
As sea cucumbers sip on brine.

A whale cracks jokes, making us roar,
While dolphins dive, shouting 'Encore!'
Starfish with dreams of Broadway fame,
Practice their lines, and play the game.

Kelp forests swing with a wacky twist,
Seagulls join in, with a funny list.
Tide pools shimmer, reflecting the fun,
How can the ocean be anything but a pun?

With laughter in bubbles, the sea does sing,
Underwater, chaos is a delightful fling.
So join in the frolic, embrace the cheer,
For in the watery depths, humor is near.

Calm After the Storm

After the storm, the sea is a tease,
Shells pop open, just like little keys.
Waves whisper softly, 'It's time to play',
Fish wear party hats, hip-hip-hooray!

Seagulls laugh, surfing on a breeze,
Wiggling their tails like they aim to please.
A sunken ship now a carousel ride,
As sea creatures party, with nothing to hide.

Tides take a break, the humor's afloat,
While barnacles dance on a rocking boat.
The waves chuckle softly, as crabs play their game,
With every splash, there's laughter to claim.

So rest on the shore, let the waves hum,
In this watery world, goodness will come.
For after the storm, life's a sparkling spree,
With joy in the tides, oh, wild and free!

Rhapsody of the Breathless Shore

Seagulls dance on the breeze,
Chasing each other's tails with ease.
Crabs hold a chorus of sideways flair,
As the sand tickles toes without a care.

Waves hum a tune to the sun's bright grin,
While fish swim by in a cheeky spin.
Starfish wear crowns of seaweed proud,
In this kingdom, the laughter is loud.

Beach balls bounce with a gleeful shout,
As children run fast, with splashes about.
The sun dips low, the sky turns pink,
Surfers fall off, and we all just wink.

We gather for snacks; a picnic delight,
As crabs do ballet under the moonlight.
With shells as our treasures, we laugh and play,
At the breathless shore, it's a silly ballet.

The Whispering Depths

Bubbles bubble in secretive glee,
As fish gossip in nautical spree.
A whale takes a cough, it echoes wide,
Jellyfish giggle as they glide.

Octopuses juggle with keen delight,
Playing hide and seek with an anchor's light.
Turtles wear hats made of sea foam,
In the whispering depths, they feel at home.

Mermen strum harps made of seaweed strands,
While crabs throw a party on soft sandy lands.
The treasure they find? Just old flip-flops,
Yet the laughter here never stops.

In depths of laughter, no frowns can dwell,
As the ocean winks in a watery spell.
A treasure of joy, deep down we dive,
In this world beneath, we come alive.

Interlude of the Sunlit Sea

In the sunlit sea, where waves love to play,
A dolphin shows off in a splashy display.
Sandy shores echo a laugh or two,
As the tide brings in stories, all shiny and new.

Clams tell tall tales of the ones who roam,
While plankton dance underneath the foam.
Seashells sing sweetly, a rhythm divine,
In this sunlit realm, everything's fine.

Walruses wobble on rocks with a cheer,
And every splash sounds like music to hear.
The sun smiles warmly on all it can see,
In this hilarious play of the sunlit sea.

With waves that giggle and grains that tease,
Every moment here brings gleeful ease.
Joy floats along with the breeze so spry,
In this sunny saga, we surely fly.

Chords in the Current

The current hums tunes of wavy delight,
As fish band together for a jam every night.
Anemones sway to a jazzy refrain,
While sea cucumbers do the conga with gain.

Bubbles bounce like notes in a lively score,
With octopuses tapping on shells at the shore.
The starfish kick back, applauding the show,
In this underwater concert, they're all in the flow.

Turtles wear shades, swaying slow like a groove,
Crabs clap their claws—look at them move!
The tide rolls in with a rhythmic cheer,
Creating a magic we all hold dear.

So let's raise our shells to this watery jam,
With laughter and music like eggs and ham.
In currents of joy, we all take a chance,
As the ocean invites us to dance-dance-dance.

Whispers of the Tide

The seagulls scream in playful jest,
With fishy jokes that never rest.
The crabs in suits, they dance around,
On sandy stages, they rebound.

A dolphin's flip, a splashing cheer,
"Hey, watch me! I've got no fear!"
As barnacles gossip, small fish snicker,
The ocean's humor flows much quicker.

A jellyfish floats, a wobbly sight,
With tentacles swaying left and right.
"Don't touch my stinger, I'm a cool dude!"
"Just passing by, don't be so rude!"

Crabby complaints and bubbles of laughter,
Each wave a chuckle, from here to after.
Together they sing, a nautical choir,
In this watery world, where joy won't tire.

Symphony of Waves

The waves crash hard, they bring a sound,
Like clumsy kids on playground ground.
A surfboard slips, a rider flies,
Splashing and laughing, oh what a prize!

The starfish dons a hat so wide,
While ocean critters watch with pride.
"Who wore it best?" they thrash and tease,
In saltwater laughter carried by the breeze.

A whale blows bubbles, it starts to hum,
As playful seals all beat the drum.
With every surge, the fun feels free,
In this quirky sea of comedy.

Tides tickle toes, a crab sings low,
"Keep your pants on, don't take a throw!"
Between the mists, excitement roams,
Where silliness in every wave freely combs.

Serenade Beneath the Surface

Fish in tuxedos swim at ease,
Complaining softly of the bees.
"I'm perfectly fine, nothing to wear!"
"Oh look, here comes a grizzly bear!"

An octopus mutters, trying a wink,
"Don't mind my colors, what do you think?"
With eight arms waving, it steals the scene,
In this underwater comedy, all is serene.

A clam plays it cool, a royal guard,
While mischievous shrimp dance quite hard.
"Let's throw a bash for the old sea bed,
And convince the waves to join instead!"

With each gurgle, laughter rings,
In hidden caverns where fun springs.
Creatures unite, as stories unfold,
In the blue depths, humor bold.

Melodies of the Deep Blue

A turtle hums a silly tune,
Bubbly laughter from a loony lagoon.
"Where's my swimming cap, I can't recall!"
"I think your head is the cap, after all!"

A fish with glasses reads the news,
"Word on the reef, we've lost our shoes!"
With fins flapping, the gossip flows,
Who knew that fish could wear such clothes?

A sandcastle falls, it's quite a sight,
"Oh dear, the tide's in for a fight!"
As crabs scurry with buckets and spades,
Making sand sculptures that surely fade.

In currents of fun, they twist and shout,
With waves that giggle and foam about.
In this underwater world, so bright and free,
Every splash and giggle, a grand decree!

Breezes and Ballads

A seagull swoops with flair,
Singing tunes without a care.
It steals my chips, oh dear,
While dolphins giggle near.

Waves are dancing, oh so spry,
A crab in shades runs by.
With every splash, a splashy laugh,
As fish join in the raucous half.

The sun wears a big, silly hat,
While octopuses prance like that.
A beach ball rolls, then takes a leap,
While sandcastles begin to weep.

So let us cheer the tidal tease,
A beachside concert, if you please!
With laughter riding every wave,
The sea's a show, come join and rave!

Waters of Wonder

Splashing sounds and friendly shouts,
Jellyfish in swim trunks flout.
Crabs are breakdancing on the sand,
While narwhals form a funky band.

Seashells play their secret tunes,
As starfish dance beneath the moons.
A whale with style, it takes the lead,
While mermaids gossip, yes indeed!

The ocean's floor, a stage so bright,
With clams applauding, what a sight!
Pirate fish with hats so grand,
Perform their acts throughout the sand.

So join the fun of sea life's jest,
Where waves and giggles are the best!
In waters deep, where laughter glows,
Adventure waits where the current flows.

Serenade for Sea Creatures

A lobster plays the accordion,
While seaweed sways to the fun.
The fish line-dance, oh so bright,
Underwater disco lights!

Turtles sport their sunglasses cool,
As seahorses splash in the pool.
They sing of ships and treasure maps,
While dolphins try on silly caps.

The octopus twirls with grace and flair,
Spraying bubbles high in the air.
Each fin and flipper in the groove,
In this underwater move!

So raise a toast to sea-life cheer,
Fishy tunes you'll want to hear!
With every splash, let's twirl and sway,
In the sea's grand cabaret!

Castaway Chorus

A parrot squawks a cheerful rhyme,
As castaways make friends with time.
They build a raft from driftwood scraps,
While crabs kick back and share some naps.

With coconuts for clinking cheers,
They toast to all their wacky years.
A turtle lends an ear to hear,
As everyone joins in good cheer!

Their songs of woe turn into laughs,
As sea urchins draw silly graphs.
And when the tide begins to roll,
The waves groove in, and they lose control!

So castaways sing, hands in the air,
To the rhythm of salty, flowing hair.
In the heart of the blue, where fun does roam,
These stranded souls have found their home!

Ode to the Open Sea

Oh look at that fish in a striped suit,
It dances so fine, in a seaweed hoot.
With bubbles as bass and sea foam cheer,
Does that fish have a lobster for a peer?

The jellyfish are throwing a party tonight,
With glow sticks a-bouncing, they're quite a sight.
A crab in a tux, oh what a delight,
He's serving up snacks with sheer seafood fright.

A dolphin in shades, surfing the tide,
With a wink and a flip, it's laughter we ride.
The sea's full of jesters, it's all in good fun,
Who knew the deep blue could be such a pun?

So raise up a toast with kelp on your plate,
Dance with the waves, don't let it be late.
For the ocean's a friend, quirky and bright,
In this splashy arena, we dance through the night.

Cadence of the Calm

A snail in a shell, what a leisurely stroll,
It's moving so slow, it's lost all control.
The turtles are chuckling, "What's the rush?"
While gulls in the sky create quite the hush.

A starfish reclines on a sunken log,
Sipping some seaweed, a charming little cog.
The sea cucumbers twirl, oh what a scene,
Catching the rays, while the fish intervene.

Seashells are gossiping about the deep,
Rumors of mermaids that simply can't leap.
"It's a wave!" shouts a clam, "A grand tidal wave!"
But turns out, just foam—a faux sea rave!

So we'll sway with the breeze, dancing on sand,
In this wacky world, life's simply unplanned.
Let's stir the salt air with laughter and cheer,
For the calm of the sea brings joy ever near.

Soft Symphony of Waves

The waves whisper secrets to sandy shores,
While crabs strut about in their tiny chores.
"Look at me!" they say, with a pinchy advance,
Yet slip on a shell in their frantic dance!

Seagulls are laughing, a chorus so bright,
They squawk and they dive, what a comical flight.
A sea horse tiptoes through kelp on a spree,
In a world full of giggles, oh can't you see?

A surfboard is wobbling, with no rider in sight,
It's just a lone fish that's put up a fight.
With a flip and a twist, it waves with great glee,
In this symphony, everyone's carefree!

So let's join in the frolic, from sunrise to set,
In this comic ballet, there's no cause for fret.
The soft waves will sing, with each gentle swell,
And laughter will echo, that's the purpose, as well.

Soundtrack of the Seaside

With a plinky plank, the barnacles jam,
While the clams tap along—what a sweet clam!
A walrus in shades croons a funny old tune,
As the tide rolls in under the light of the moon.

The flounders are flopping, feet tapping with glee,
As dolphins play tag in a bubbly spree.
The seaweed sways gently, a dancer so prime,
In this quirky ocean, everyone's in time!

Oh, the soundtrack here brings a laugh to us all,
With a twist, a shimmy, and a cannonball.
Fish sing in bubbles, the octopus claps,
As the sun dips low, it's all laughter and laps!

So let's bounce with the waves, join the aquatic throng,
In this merry maritime, where we all belong.
With a splash on the scene, let the fun never cease,
For in salty-filled laughter, we find our peace.

Dreaming with Dorsal Fins

Fins and tales beneath the waves,
Where fish spin songs in playful caves.
The octopus winks, a clownfish grins,
As seaweed dances, the party begins.

Seahorses strut in their tiny suits,
While dolphins show off their silly hoots.
A crab does the twist with a shake of claw,
And jellyfish glide with a wobbly awe.

Starfish join in with a wobbly jig,
While turtles ponder, 'Do we dance big?'
The sea foam laughs as it tickles the shore,
In this underwater realm, who could ask for more?

So plunge to the depths, leave worries at bay,
Join the fish party, it's a fin-tastic day!
With bubbles of joy and laughter afloat,
In this wild ocean dance, let's all rock the boat!

Horizon's Enchantment

At dawn, the sun yawns, a big orange round,
As gulls drop by for a snack on the ground.
The waves chuckle softly, a tickle for toes,
While mermaids gossip in seashells, I suppose.

A whale in a top hat, so dapper and neat,
Struts by the beach, what a curious feat!
With each splash and giggle, the tide takes a bow,
As crabs turn to tap dance, oh wow, look at them now!

The horizon whispers with salty delight,
As waves play peek-a-boo, a fantastic sight.
Seagulls guffaw while they chase a lost fry,
In this sea of enchantment, I just can't deny.

Summer jesters splash water, they cheer and they play,
With a flip and a flail, they brighten the day.
Laughter rides waves, flips surfboards, off we go,
In this world of whimsy, it's a splashy show!

Treasure Beneath the Surface

Pirates giggle with pots of gold,
But really, it's shells that are special and bold.
With every dive, a secret awaits,
Like a fish dressed in polka dots, oh what fun traits!

Crabs hide treasures, like shiny old spoons,
While mermaids sing silly, off-key tunes.
The anchor's a throne for a munchy sea snail,
As seafloor dancers spin tales of their trails.

Divers discover a jellyfish jest,
Who's wearing a crown, looking fancy and blessed.
The seaweed giggles, the corals all sway,
In the depths of this humor, let's dive and just play.

Joy wrapped in bubbles, twirls in the foam,
In this quirky seascape, we twirl and we roam.
What wonders await in the heart of the deep?
It's a treasure of laughter, a promise we keep!

Tidal Tones

The tide rolls in like a playful prank,
With splashes that sing from a wobbly tank.
Shells percussive, they beat on the shore,
While fish hold a concert, we crave even more.

Waves crash like laughter, a merry-go-round,
Dancing with dolphins, lost joy can be found.
The sand's a soft stage for crabs to perform,
Cranking out rhythms while they entertain norm.

Seagulls strut, making whispers of sound,
As beach-goers giggle, casting joy all around.
With every breeze, there's a chuckle or two,
In this chorus of fun, there's a song just for you.

So let's leap with joy as the tide rolls on by,
And twirl with the waves, oh, time will just fly!
For laughter and music pretty much blend,
In this silly tide dance with joy as our friend.

Tides of Time: A Coastal Tale

The waves bring tales from afar,
Of fish who dream of becoming a star.
A crab in a tux sprinkles his flair,
While seagulls play tricks, all unaware.

The clam joins a dance, all shy and sweet,
Wobbling around on its tiny feet.
With laughter that echoes like splashes at sea,
These silly creatures grow more carefree.

A starfish tries yoga, oh what a sight!
Stretching its limbs with all of its might.
The jellyfish giggles, floats by with glee,
As the tides hold their breath, just wait and see.

So here's to the fun that the coast always brings,
With crabby conspirators and silly little things.
A frothy sea swirl, a laugh or a cheer,
In the waves of the water, all worries disappear.

Currents of Silvery Light

A fish with a hat swims by with pride,
Spreading its fins, on a watery slide.
It winks at a dolphin, a buddy so bright,
Who's flipping and twisting, in pure delight.

The sunbeams giggle, they dance on the crest,
As crabs don their sunglasses, making a nest.
A seaweed party, where everyone claps,
While a clam spills the punch, all hands in laps.

Octopuses juggling, oh what a show!
With eight arms fluttering, putting on a glow.
The currents are laughing, the waves roll with cheer,
In this lighthearted world, there's nothing to fear.

So dive into laughter, feel the fun swell,
In the shimmering depths where the good vibes dwell.
Let the tides take you high, let the bubbles rise,
In the shine of the sea, where humor never dies.

The Dance of the Solitary Ship

A lonely boat wobbles on waves so wide,
With a flag that flutters, full of boat pride.
It spins and it twirls, a sailor's ballet,
While seagulls around it, call out, 'Hey, hey!'

Its captain's a cat, with a patch on one eye,
Counting fish with a sigh, as they swim by.
With a wink and a nod, the old boat sets sail,
Bouncing on ripples, telling sea tales.

But oh, what's this? A school of fish leap!
In a whirl of colors, they dance, oh so neat.
The cat joins the fun, with a whisker-twitch cheer,
As the ship sways along, nothing seems to fear.

In a spin, in a loop, they twist and they turn,
Each wave brings a laugh, a joy we can learn.
Embrace the silly, feel the splash and flip,
In the dance of the sea, on this solo ship.

Songs of Shell and Starfish

In a world by the shore, shells gather in glee,
Each one is a story, wild as can be.
A conch sings of travels, through sand and through foam,
While starfish keep time to this melodic roam.

The seagulls engage in a comedic act,
Pretending to dance, with each funny fact.
A hermit crab drums, using shells on the ground,
Creating a rhythm where laughter is found.

The tides start to hum, a tune full of mirth,
As waves hug the sand, sharing secrets of earth.
With shells as their instruments, they play all day long,
In this jubilant orchestra, no one feels wrong.

So join in the laughter, let your heart sing bright,
With a splash and a giggle, under stars of the night.
In the shell and the sea, the joy never fades,
As we dance with the tide, and its playful parades.

Lullabies of the Seafloor

In the deep blue, fish sing tunes,
While dancing squids act like buffoons.
Crabs tap dance on the sandy stage,
Shouting, 'Join us for a seaweed rage!'

Starfish stretch like yoga pros,
Jellyfish jiggle, striking poses.
Seashells gossip in playful glee,
Waves giggle back, 'Oh, let it be!'

Octopus plays hide and seek,
Inking jokes, but not to tweak.
Shrimp tell tales of their wild nights,
While dolphins tease with acrobatic flights.

Sea cucumbers, shy and meek,
Whisper secrets that make you squeak.
In this realm where giggles swell,
Marine mischief casts a spell!

Echoes of the Briny Abyss

Underwater echoes take the floor,
A fish named Bob always wants more.
'Hey, whale, sing that one again!'
But the whale just shrugged with a grin.

Turtles confused in a racing spree,
Thought they'd won, but just drank tea.
Seal pups rolling, slipping and sliding,
While a clam complains about tides subsiding.

Crabby crabs with pinch-a-lot tricks,
Boast of gem-studded seashell picks.
Mermaids laugh under the moonglow,
As sea urchins thump to the flow.

Bubbles rise with hilarity,
Creating quite the merry parody.
From coral reefs to floating debris,
Funny echoes shout, 'Come dance with me!'

Ballad of the Breaking Surf

Waves crash down, but who's surprised?
A gull swoops low, with food disguised.
Surfboards fly like frisky birds,
While stargazers sing giggly words.

Sandy toes and playful pranks,
Kids build castles, drawing chanks.
A flip-flop lands on a fishy face,
'Whoa, dude, this is no beachy race!'

Seagulls squawking with big-crab sass,
Try to snatch a tasty piece of grass.
Surf bunnies bounce with glee and flair,
While surfing squid are quite the pair.

Laughter rings as the tide pulls near,
A sea snail races; 'Watch me, dear!'
In the curls of foam, a jester's dance,
Ocean's laughter gives you a chance!

Harmony of the Horizon

At dawn, fish wear their happy coats,
While mermaids hum cheeky notes.
Crashing waves harmonize in glee,
As starry night plays hide and seek.

Seagulls dive after giggly snacks,
While dolphins leap, racing lax.
Turtles munch on seaweed bites,
Plotting pranks with the moonlit nights.

A whale winks from afar, so bright,
Challenging anyone to surf the night.
And the sunset melts in colorful hues,
As fish gather round for a joyful snooze.

Bubbles burst with jolly cheer,
Creating echoes for all to hear.
Ocean's jesters never stop,
Inventing laughter, a never-ending prop!

The Rhythm of Raindrops

Raindrops dance on the pavement,
Tap-tap-tap to their own beat,
Puddles splash with a giggle,
As kids jump in, oh what a treat!

Umbrellas flip like fish in the air,
People run like they're in a race,
One slips and falls, without a care,
Covered in soggy shoe lace!

Clouds rumble with a chuckling sound,
As lightning strikes a silly pose,
Nature's comedian, joy is found,
In each drop, fun overload grows!

So let us dance in rain's embrace,
Sing along to its whimsical tune,
For every storm leaves a smiling face,
And a rainbow shines at noon!

Aria of the Anchors

Anchors aweigh, but who took the bait?
A seagull squawks, it's getting quite late,
Ship's bell rings with a clang and a pop,
Captain's hat flies, who's calling a stop?

Sailors leap like fish out of line,
Tangled in ropes, oh, what a design!
One trips on a bucket, the crew starts to laugh,
As waves clap their hands for this silly gaffe!

Mermaids peek from the foam with delight,
They giggle beneath the moon's shining light,
While crabs hold their claws, preparing to dance,
Joining in the fun with a clammy romance!

So grab your oars, let's row out with glee,
For under the sun, we're wild and free,
The ocean waves bring a tune so bright,
Tan lines and laughter, oh, what a sight!

Vocal Waves

Waves sing a tune, with splashes and froth,
They tickle the shore, then dash back off,
Seashells join in, resounding a cheer,
The beach is our stage, come lend me your ear!

A crab decides to break into dance,
With claws held high and a wobbly prance,
Starfish claps, with a wink and a spin,
While dolphins jump in, let the rhymes begin!

Flip-flops flapping like a chorus of birds,
Beach towels flutter, singing their words,
Sandcastles stand proud, beaming with pride,
Under this symphony, let joy be our guide!

So let's surf along these melodic waves,
With laughter and fun, we're the ocean's brave,
Together we'll harmonize, dance with the tide,
In this funny concert, we all take a ride!

Serenade of Shells

Shells whisper secrets of distant lands,
Gathered by waves and teenage hands,
A conch takes center stage for a tune,
While daisies sway in the afternoon.

Clams tell stories of pirates' old loot,
While oystercatchers dance in pursuit,
Crabs tap their claws like jazz in the sun,
Each melody played is filled with fun!

A starfish croons beneath the bright light,
While children laugh, their spirits take flight,
Dune parades set their colorful sights,
As the shells join in, quantum delights!

So gather your friends, make footprints in sand,
For a concert of laughter, it's oh so grand,
In this shell-laden world, we sing and we sway,
Forever enchanted by sunlit play!

Fragments of Dawn on the Deep

The sunrise winks on waves so bright,
Fish wear sunglasses, oh what a sight!
Seagulls dance in their skimpy attire,
While crabs throw a bash by a bonfire.

Turtles surf down the coral slides,
Dolphins giggle and take us for rides.
Starfish are twirling, looking so spry,
Who knew the sea was a party up high?

Shells trade gossip of treasures untold,
While seaweed scolds them for being so bold.
An octopus juggles with flair and grace,
While the clownfish laugh in their colorful space.

As night falls down, the mermaids convene,
Belly flops make quite the aquatic scene.
In bubbles they whisper, with laughter they float,
What a wild party on this big blue boat!

Vignettes of the Blue Refuge

In the shallows, a crab wears a hat,
A tiny tuxedo, imagine that!
Fish throw confetti with bubbles galore,
And sea cucumbers roll on the floor.

Anemones dance in the gentle sway,
While dolphins tell jokes in a splashy display.
Shrimp join the chorus, a chorus of cheer,
What a funny neighborhood down here!

Clownfish snicker as they play peek-a-boo,
Sea turtles ponder what to do.
With jellyfish waltzing, it's quite the affair,
They laugh at the sun, without a care.

At dusk, the light fades with a shimmering glow,
Lobsters parade, making quite the show.
As stars twinkle brightly above our blue home,
They sing serenades across ocean foam!

Ballad of the Seafoam Dreams

Bubbles giggle as they drift with glee,
An octopus dreams of cracking a spree.
Seashells collect stories, oh what delight,
As crabs boast their talents and dance in the night.

A fish in a bow tie leads a grand ball,
A shrimp joins the limbo, and yes, he stands tall!
While puffers inflate, they think it's a game,
What a ruckus they make — they should feel some shame.

Starfish play tag on the sandy floor,
While jellyfish float through the ocean's decor.
Dolphins in sunglasses flip through the waves,
Making the most of their frolicsome caves.

As day turns to night, the fun finds its end,
With laughter and giggles, on each wave they send.
The sea's full of nonsense, a lighthearted spree,
While dreams drift along with the tide, wild and free!

Tidepool Echoes

In tidepools, friends are a quirky bunch,
Crabs play hopscotch in their seafood lunch.
Starfish contemplate life at their own pace,
While sea urchins poke at the morning's grace.

Clownfish juggle tiny pearls with flair,
Seahorses ride waves in a style so rare.
Little hermit crabs strut with great pride,
In suits made of shells, they're the talk of the tide.

Flatfish hide with sneaky delight,
Pretending they're rocks, oh what a sight!
And octopuses change from blue to bright pink,
As they share their secrets with dolphins that wink.

As the tide whispers soft tales of cheer,
Every whispering wave brings the laughter near.
The ocean is playful, a curious land,
Full of joy and oddities so grand!

The Heartbeat of the Harbor

Waves dance and splash, like kids at play,
Seagulls squawk loudly, in their own ballet.
A lobster wore shades, looking so cool,
While fish all giggled, "What a silly fool!"

The boats all bob, like drunkards at sea,
One tipped its hat, shouting, "Look at me!"
Crabs play the banjo, a tune full of cheer,
While octopuses juggle with no trace of fear!

Mermaids on break, sipping sea-salt shakes,
Sing off-key, causing some serious quakes.
"What's your favorite dish?" a fishy friend asked,
"Just anything fried, that's all that I've basked!"

The harbor's alive, with laughter and fun,
A watery circus under the sun.
Whales do the limbo, dolphins dive low,
In this raucous place, smiles steal the show!

Lull of the Longshore

The waves whisper secrets, tickling the sand,
A crab makes a sandcastle, looking quite grand.
The tide rolls in, with a mischievous grin,
As seaweed wigs dance, and the laughter begins.

A clam tells its story, a tale quite absurd,
Of pirates with treasure, who never occurred.
Seagulls play poker, chips scattered like shells,
While jellyfish flash, casting amusing spells.

The sun sets slowly, dripping like honey,
As sea turtles chuckle, so sweet and so funny.
The night's sea breeze carries chuckles and glee,
While fish tell tall tales of wild jubilee.

Fishermen snooze, wrapped in nets and yarn,
Dreaming of mermaids by the light of the barn.
As the stars shimmer brightly, the ocean does sway,
In this lull of the longshore, we laugh till the day.

Tides of Time

The waves roll in with a clamor and cheer,
Like a marching band, sounding loud and clear.
A starfish reclines, sipping a fizzy drink,
While crabs practice ballet, taking a wink.

Chronicles told by the shells on the shore,
Of fish who ran shops, and that's just the score.
"Who needs a watch?" said a whale with a smile,
"Just count all the tides; it'll take you a while!"

The gulls played chess on a board made of sand,
While dolphins played tag, what a goofy band!
The rhythm of waves, with a quirky embrace,
Is a timeless melody, tickling our face.

So as the sands shift, and the tides come and go,
Each laughter-filled moment starts putting on a show.
In the dance of the tides, there's a wink and a grin,
A symphony of joy, where laughter begins!

Lament of the Lighthouse Keeper

High atop the rocks, the keeper laments,
"A gull stole my sandwich—such lacks common sense!"
The light spins around, while the foghorn does moan,
"Why can't I just work in a big taco zone?"

With starfish as friends and a crab on his hat,
He argues with seagulls who argue right back.
"Yo ho, matey!" a fish inquires loud,
"Why not just give up? Just float with the crowd!"

He waxes the lantern, sighing in despair,
As dolphins parade, without any care.
"What's wrong with this world?" he yells at the breeze,
"Those fish mock my wits; please put me at ease!"

Yet when night falls down, and the sea sparkles bright,
He chuckles and thinks, "Oh, this sure feels right!"
With laughter and stories, he guards the bay light,
In the lighthouse of mischief, all's merry tonight.

Ripples of Reflection

A crab in a tux, so dapper and neat,
Dances on sand with quick little feet.
The seagulls complain, they squawk and they flail,
While fish in the waves just laugh at the tale.

The shore has a grin, all sprinkled with cream,
As waves toss around like a bubbly dream.
A starfish is posing, a true fashionista,
Saying, "Who needs a beach when you have a fiesta?"

Flip-flops are flinging, socks lost in the tide,
While clams throw a party, their pearls are their pride.
And when the tide tugs, they tumble and roll,
A circus of shells, they're taking a stroll.

So here comes the sun, with a wink and a smile,
Not one single dolphin will swim for a while.
For laughter is ringing, the waves are in sync,
In this sea of jest, there's no time to think.

Deep Blue Reverie

A fish with a hat, he's ready to dive,
Says, "Life's like a party, let's keep it alive!"
The jellyfish jiggles, so smooth and so bright,
While plankton do waltzes, under moon's light.

A turtle in shades, too cool for the day,
Glides past with a grin, as he sways in the spray.
Octopuses juggle, their arms full of fun,
In this aquatic world, who needs the sun?

The bubbles keep popping, a symphony first,
Each giggle and gurgle, a joyful burst.
While seaweed is twirling, a soft, leafy dance,
With every wave crashing, they whisper, "Take a chance!"

And when the tide giggles, it's hard not to cheer,
With water so buoyant, it tickles the ear.
Just ride on this surf, with a chuckle or two,
In this deep blue realm, where joy is the glue.

Harmonies of the Horizon

A whale sings a tune, a cheeky old croon,
While dolphins jump high, enjoying the moon.
The waves clink like glasses, in cheerful delight,
As fish throw confetti, to celebrate night.

The sand giggles softly, feeling so spry,
It tickles your toes as you pass it by.
Crabs in their chorus, creating a beat,
As they march to the rhythm, with pinching feet!

Seaweed sways gently, in the breeze's embrace,
As shells form a choir, in shimmering grace.
A shoal of bright colors swims past with a laugh,
While barnacles join in, to make a grand staff.

And when the tide winks, it whispers a jest,
"Come dance with the currents, and take a deep rest!"
For here in this haven, where humor runs deep,
You'll find all the laughter, the ocean can keep.

Coral Chimes

In a reef of bright colors, a clownfish tries jokes,
While sponges roll their eyes and share silly pokes.
A seahorse in spectacles, wise with a glare,
Says, "Laughter is key, let's spread joy everywhere!"

A group of shy anemones start to sway,
As corals declare it's a funny play day.
With every soft ripple, a giggle takes flight,
While barnacles crack up, it's quite the sight!

The king of the sea, with a crown made of shells,
Shares tales of his court, where humor compels.
With a wave and a flick, they all join in tune,
To the rhythm of laughter, beneath the bright moon.

So come join the chorus, don't be shy, my friend,
With fins all a-flutter, let's laugh without end.
For in this grand symphony, where all creatures sing,
Each chuckle and chime makes the ocean bling!

www.ingramcontent.com/pod-product-compliance
Lightning Source LLC
Chambersburg PA
CBHW072218070526
44585CB00015B/1388